HANDBOOK

THE CHRISTIAN BABY-SITTER'S HANDBOOK

By Sarah Fletcher
Illustrated by Chris Sharp

CPH

SAINT LOUIS

Copyright © 1985, 1997 Concordia Publishing House
3558 S. Jefferson Avenue, St. Louis, MO 63118-3968
Manufactured in the United States of America

Library of Congress Cataloging-in-Publication Data

Fletcher, Sarah.
      The Christian babysitter's handbook/Sarah Fletcher.—New ed.
        p.   cm.
      Originally published: St. Louis: Concordia, 1985.
      ISBN 0-570-04889-3
      1. Baby-sitting—Handbooks, manuals, etc.—Juvenile literature.
  2. Baby-sitters—Juvenile literature. 3. Youth—Religious life—Juvenile literature. 4. Christian education of children—Juvenile literature. I. Title.
HQ769.5.F54 1997
649'.1'0248—dc20   96-43745

2 3 4 5 6 7 8 9 10   06 05 04 03 02 01 00 99 98

*For all the baby-sitters
who love their jobs*

Contents

1

So, You're a Christian Baby-sitter ...

How do you feel about that?

Maybe you've never baby-sat before. In that case, your stomach may feel a little like an elevator without any brakes.

That's understandable. After all, you're suddenly switching roles in a big way. Until now, other people have been taking care of you. Now *you're* the one who will be taking care of others.

What kind of pictures do you see in your mind? Long, empty hours that you somehow have to fill before you can put the kids to bed? A huge, creaky house with prowlers peeking through every window and emergencies lurking around every corner?

Or, are you remembering all the things *you* used to do to hapless baby-sitters? (Be sure, your sins will find you out!)

Don't worry. The pages ahead will give you some ideas not only for filling those long hours, but also for making them good ones for both you and the children. We'll talk about how to handle emergencies too—should any emerge.

And you might even learn a trick or two that *your* baby-sitters didn't know.

Then again, maybe you aren't nervous at all. Maybe you've baby-sat a lot in the past and are frankly just a little bored with the whole thing.

Read on anyway. What you need is a fresh outlook. And there's no better outlook than to realize that what you're doing is honest-to-goodness Christian ministry.

And that brings us to the key question. Does being a *Christian* baby-sitter make any difference?

Does it ever! It makes a difference in how you feel about you, how you feel about the kids, and how you feel about what you're doing.

In fact, as God's Holy Spirit helps you celebrate the fact that Jesus gave His life to win you new life, being a Christian makes a difference in your whole life—including baby-sitting.

2
What's Baby-sitting?

Well, it doesn't always mean babies. Sometimes you'll be taking care of older kids—and you'd better not call them babies, at least not when they can hear you.

Baby-sitting doesn't always mean sitting either. Sometimes—like when you're giving Michael his 14th horsey ride or fishing around under the king-size bed for Ashley's lost teddy bear—you'll wish you *could* do a little more sitting.

No, what baby-sitting means is that for a period of time, you are responsible for the lives of one or more of God's children. Does that sound like serious stuff? It is. But that doesn't mean baby-sitting can't be fun—and rewarding too.

But before we get to the fun and rewards,

think for a moment about the word *responsible*. It comes from the word *respond*. You must be able to *respond* to the needs of the children you're watching. You must be able to *respond* to their parents' expectation that you'll do a good job. And you must be able to *respond* to God's will for you.

How did *God* get into all this? That's simple. He *has* called you—and all other Christians—to actively serve Him. It's right there in 1 Peter: But you are a chosen people, a royal priesthood, a holy nation, a people belonging to God, that you may declare the praises of Him who called you out of darkness into His wonderful light (1 Peter 2:9).

Being God's servant is a full-time job. It gets mixed up in every part of your life. And it often means that you end up serving Him by serving His people—including the children you baby-sit.

Now, just because you're a responsible child of God doesn't mean you have to go around looking like a moldy prune. It doesn't mean you have to march around like a five-star general either.

You can be responsible and have fun too. You can play with the kids and laugh at their silliness. You can even get pretty silly yourself.

But at the same time, one part of you

must always remember: I'm in charge here. I've got to feel on top of things—all the time.

If you can balance those two things—responsibility and fun—then baby-sitting will bring you some rewards that are even better than the money you'll earn.

You might get a phone call from a parent who says, "Can you come next Friday night? We'd rather have you than anyone else."

Or, you might be tucking in a cover and suddenly hear a sleepy little voice say, "I love you."

Or, best of all, you might know that special feeling deep inside that comes when God is saying to you, "Servant, well done!"

3

Getting a Job (If That's Your Problem)

If it isn't your problem—if you've got as many baby-sitting jobs as you can handle—skip this chapter.

Or, consider opening your own sitters' agency. It's been done before. What you do is promise to provide responsible sitters for parents who need them—and jobs for responsible sitters. Then you either charge the parents a small fee or take a small percentage of what the sitters earn. Once again, though, the key word is *responsible*.

But suppose you *are* responsible, ready, and eager to baby-sit, and no one asks you. How can you make the phone start ringing? Fear not. Your condition is only temporary.

The parents with jobs to offer are out there. And they're probably as ready and eager as you are.

The secret is to let them know you're there. Nobody's going to buy a super new invention if it's hidden away in a warehouse somewhere. And nobody's going to hire the services of a sitter they don't know has those services to sell.

So stop hiding your light under a bushel. Advertise! You might start by talking to friends who already do a lot of baby-sitting. Ask them to recommend you for the jobs they can't take. Ask your parents and older friends to mention your new career to *their* friends too.

Make a list of neighbors with small children. Then give them each a call or hand them each a flyer to tell them you're going into business. Parents usually like having a sitter in the neighborhood. It makes transportation so much easier.

Another effective way to advertise is by putting a card on the bulletin board at your church. (Better get permission from the church office or your pastor before you do this, though.) Keep the card simple—and neat. A brightly colored border around the card wouldn't hurt either.

RESPONSIBLE
BABY-SITTER
wants jobs—
Call EMILY EAGER
555-5555

With all that advertising—and a little patience—you should soon have all the sitting jobs you can handle. Then *you* can start thinking about opening an agency.

4
Here I Am!

It's come at last—that first baby-sitting job. Or, perhaps it's just your first job with a new family. In either case, you walk in the door and see a dressed-up adult or two smiling at you. You see a couple of wide-eyed children peering at you.

You walk in the door and what do *they* see? A girl with her hair in rollers or a boy with grease under his fingernails? A kid with the posture of a limp pretzel or with elbows poking out of the world's oldest sweatshirt?

Heaven forbid!

True, on the inside you may be a beautiful person. But facts are also facts. And it's a fact that when you're making a first impression, outsides matter—a lot.

Of course you don't have to dress as if you're about to be presented at Buckingham Palace. But you don't have to look like a refugee from a horror film either. Wear something clean and neat—something that makes you look like the responsible person you are.

Then there's the matter of manners. A polite "Yes, ma'am" or "No, sir" never hurt anyone. Good manners also tend to make parents think like this: H-m-m-m. Obviously that kid has been well raised. A kid like that should do a good job with *our* kids.

Besides, good manners really are linked up to the heart, manners are a way of acting out how we feel about people. And that's a way of living out the love God gives to us in Jesus.

Finally, there's attitude. You've got one and it's good. You're serving God's people, and you're going to do the best, most responsible job you can. But how can you make the family you're working for see that?

Well, attitudes are partly communicated through the things we've already mentioned—dress, posture, manners. But there are other ways you can show your attitude too.

Show interest in the children right away. Remember, they're probably feeling unsure of you—and maybe even a little frightened.

Be warm. Use their names. A friendly, "Hi, Ben. Hey, I like your shoes. Are they new?" works a lot better than, "Well, uh, hi, uh." No one likes to be called "Uh." And almost everyone feels better when you occasionally use their name—even the dog. Show the children that you like kids right off the bat and their parents will know it too.

Another way to show the family your good attitude is by asking the right questions—the responsible questions—before the parents leave. Find out everything you need to know to do your job well. When parents see that you've thought about these things, they'll know that you're taking your job (and their children) seriously. Your good attitude will shine right through.

And what are those right questions? Read on!

5
What Do They Expect?

When you buy something, you expect certain things of it. If it's a candy bar, you expect it to taste like candy, not fish food. If it's a sweater, you expect it to keep you warm and not fall apart the first time you wash it.

When parents buy your services as a baby-sitter, they expect certain things of you. Some parents will tell you their expectations right away. But you may have to ask others a few things.

Start with food. Are you supposed to feed the kids? What do they eat and drink? Are they allowed bedtime snacks? What can they have?

Then there's bedtime itself. (As you probably know from experience, children are not always scrupulously honest on this subject.)

What is bedtime for each child? Who gets to read in bed? Who gets a night-light?

What about baths before bed? Do any of the children need help with a bath? Are there smaller children who need help using the toilet?

No one likes to think about the whole subject of child abuse. But it's real, and so you do have to think about it, especially when you are responsible for children. Clear instructions from parents as to how much help and what kind of help their children need in the bathroom will set your mind at ease.

Older children may have homework. When and where should they do it? May they stay up until it's done? How about the computer? Are there special rules for its use?

And how about chores? Who puts away the toys? clears the table? feeds the dog?

What about TV? Any rules about what the kids may or may not watch? Any limits on how much they may watch? The same questions hold true for videos and video games.

We'll talk about discipline in general later. But try to find out special family rules right away. If everyone else knows that when Molly doesn't eat her stewed prunes she doesn't get any brownie delight, then you need to know that too. If Andrew is sent to his room for a time-out every time he throws a tantrum, you'll want to handle him the same way.

Sometimes there will be special instructions about medicines or what to do if Mr. So-and-So calls. Be sure you clearly understand each instruction. *Never* give a child any sort of medicine without full parental knowledge and approval.

It's also a good idea to check out the family's religious customs before the parents leave. Do the children say grace before meals? Do they have bedtime prayers? Would they like you to listen to them say their prayers? If so, add a prayer of your own, asking God to bless the children and give them a good night's sleep.

After you've sat for a particular family several times, the parents' expectations will become second nature to you. But until then, don't be afraid to ask questions. No one will think you're a dimwit. In fact, they'll probably consider you one smart sitter!

The following checklist might help you keep track of the expectations of the various families you work for. Make as many copies of it as you need. Enlarge them if you want to keep them in a notebook. (More about notebooks later.) Or, put them in a card file. Or, if you're high-tech, enter them into your computer.

Near the end of this book, you'll find another form to help you with emergencies. Feel free to alter both forms to suit your situation. Then keep them together in a place where you can get them when you need them. Parents might appreciate having copies of the forms too.

Baby-sitter's Checklist

Family name:

_____

Address:

_____

_____

Phone number(s):

_____

_____

Names and ages of children:

_____

_____

_____

_____

Rules about food:

_____

_____

_____

_____

Times and rules for bed:

_____

_____

_____

_____

Rules about homework:

_____

_____

_____

Chores:

_____

_____

_____

_____

Rules for use of TV, computer, and other appliances:

_____

_____

_____

Bedtime stories and prayers:

_____

_____

_____

Other special rules and instructions:

_____

_____

_____

_____

6

What Can You Expect?

The parents who hired you to baby-sit aren't the only people with expectations. You are entitled to some too, and it's just as important for you to make them clear from the very beginning.

Let's start with the issue of pay. Baby-sitting rates vary a great deal from community to community. So does the way the rates are figured.

Some sitters simply charge a flat rate by the hour. Others charge more for the hours after midnight or for a special occasion, such as during the late Christmas Eve service. Still others charge additional amounts for more than one child.

Find out what the going rates and practices are among your friends. Then let your employers know what you expect. Being a Christian doesn't mean you have to be wishy-washy about pay. "Oh, well, er, anything's okay" is not a good billing practice for anyone. In fact, it can result in confused parents and (sometimes) a resentful you. "I worked here all day for *three* dollars?"

Money, though, is just one of your expectations. You certainly can expect the parents to tell you everything you need to know—including where they are going, how they can be reached while they're gone, and what time they'll be back.

Sometimes, of course, people go places where they can't easily be reached—such as to a shopping mall or a series of open houses. But even then you can expect them to give you the number of someone who can act in their place in case of emergency. (We'll go into more detail about that sort of thing later.)

You can also expect parents to come home right around the time they've said they will. Anyone can be delayed for a few minutes. But people who habitually drive in an hour or more late are taking advantage of you. And that's wrong. Scratch them off your list of employers and let them find other sitters in the future.

If parents have been to a party where

alcohol was served, at least one of them should have abstained so he or she could do the driving—including taking you home.

Never ride home with someone you think is drunk! If necessary, call your own parents and ask them to come get you. Refusing to ride with someone who is drunk isn't prudish. It's common sense. And if the parents who hired you end up embarrassed—tough! Maybe *they'll* be more responsible next time.

When you take a baby-sitting job, it is fair for you to expect that your main job will be baby-sitting. Of course you'll do your best to cope with the orange juice Jacob spilled on the cat. Of course you'll clear the supper dishes if you've fed the kids. But no one should expect you to do yesterday's breakfast dishes or the laundry that just happens to have piled up in the basement or to run the vacuum cleaner over the living room and—oh, yes—just dust around the edges a little.

There aren't many people who would even ask such things of you. But if you run into someone who does, remember that you have the right to say no (politely)—and, if necessary, to scratch them off your list.

And you'll probably find times when you *want* to do something special, when parents you've learned to like a lot have had to dash off and leave the house a mess. Then the urge to do some cleaning up may be more than you can resist. You're doing it as a gift of love. That's different.

7
The Perqs

Perqs. That's business slang for *perquisites,* the extra benefits that come with a job.

Baby-sitters get their share of perqs too. But these can vary from place to place. So it's best to know what the parents are giving before you do any taking.

One perq you'll sometimes be offered is free food. Some parents will even go so far as to say, "Eat anything in the refrigerator that looks good to you."

Then your common sense must prevail. Maybe you *can* wolf down an entire chocolate cream pie. But will your body get even with you later? And what will even the most generous of parents secretly think about you?

Other parents will be more specific. "If you get hungry, there are potato chips, soda pop, and carrot sticks." In that case, keep your grubby paws away from the pie.

A few folks may actually forget that people your age tend to munch a lot. Grin and bear the hunger pangs the first time this happens. But the next time you work there, tuck a goody from home into your pocket or purse. Just don't eat it in front of the children. That's mean!

A humongous TV with 934 fascinating channels, a complete library of video games, or some other electronic marvel may also be among the perqs you're offered. Just be sure you understand the rules governing your use of them. No fair switching off "Sesame Street" so you can watch "The Bionic Octopus." And don't mess with the family's PC unless specifically told you may. A personal computer is just that—personal.

What about having friends over while you're sitting—you know, just to keep you company? Frankly, most parents don't like that idea. They feel they've hired you to keep their kids company, and that's what they want you to do. But if some parents insist that it's okay—that they really *want* you to have someone over—be sure not to abuse the privilege.

Telephone privileges are another area where you'll want to be careful. Sometimes you just *have* to call someone to find out your math assignment or see if you got a part in the play. But always keep such calls short. You never know. The parents might be trying to call *you.* And two hours of straight busy signal could make them downright crabby.

How about naps? Is it okay if you take a little snooze after the kids are in bed? Some parents say, "Fine," especially if they plan to be out late. Others would rather you didn't. They're afraid something might go wrong—such as a child getting sick—and you might not wake up. Find out how the parents you're working for feel about sleeping on the job. Then respect their wishes.

One of the best things about sitting is that sometimes you can do two things at once—such as sit and study. That's great. But there will also be times when you can't study, when the children will demand every ounce of your attention and energy. At those times the books simply have to go.

You must never—*ever*—put any of the perqs before your job, which is taking care of the children. If you really *need* to study or spend a Saturday night with your friends or catch up on your sleep, figure that out ahead of time and don't take the baby-sitting job.

Part of servanthood is stewardship, and stewardship isn't just putting a percentage of your earnings into the collection plate each Sunday. It's also using your time, talents, and energy in the best possible way—for others and for you.

8

Kids Are People Too

Parents are an important part of your career as a baby-sitter. So, obviously, are you. But most important of all are the children. Face it, without them you'd be out of a job. Not many folks hire someone to sit with their fish.

But people—even people your age—tend to forget fast what it's like to be a kid. Some folks look down on them. They think they're just insignificant little savages who haven't grown up yet. Or, inferior beings that it's fun to order around.

These folks are wrong. Children are every bit as much God's creatures as you or I or anyone else. God's Son died and rose for them just as much as for anyone else. And no one has the right to think of them as insignificant little savages or inferior beings.

Of course other folks get so mushily carried away by how cute children can be that they expect them to behave like angels all the time.

They're wrong too. Children are sinners—just like you and me and anyone else. Dainty little Danielle may well bop the baby over the head with her doll. Curly-haired Kevin may well bite you on the knee.

Kids are people. They have feelings. Some of those feelings are good. Some aren't. It's up to you to bring out as many of the good feelings as you can.

If you act like a drill sergeant and boss kids around all the time, they're likely to burst—usually into tears or tantrums. Those aren't the kinds of feelings you want to deal with.

On the other hand, if you approach kids with all the backbone of a wet dishrag, they may try to take over. They'll defy you—or sneak around you. Those aren't the kinds of feelings you want to deal with either.

We'll get around to the matter of discipline later. But for now, it's good to remember that kids will tend to give you what you expect them to give you. Expect them to be brats and they probably won't disappoint you. Expect them to be normal, healthy, and sometimes even helpful little human beings, and that's probably what you'll get.

Speaking of helpful, sometimes kids—especially little ones—will just beg to help you clear the table, clean up the puddle, whatever. (As soon as they're old enough to be of any real help, most kids lose this impulse.) You know you could do the job better and in much less time by yourself.

But forget time. Forget quality. Generations of mothers have made the sacrifice of letting their children help them because it means so much to the helpers. Swallow your impatience and join their legions.

Kids are people. Like other people, they're all different. You have to get to know them one at a time before you can have a really good relationship with them.

Shy Suzanne may need to sit in the corner with her teddy bear for half an hour before she'll warm up to you. She'll probably burst into tears if you look at her cross-eyed. When Suzanne does something wrong, a gentle "That's not a good idea" is usually enough to stop her.

Bubba, on the other hand, charges at you like a tractor trailer the minute you arrive. The faces he can make are enough to leave *you* in tears. And you may have to be very firm just to get his attention when he does something wrong.

But different as they are, Suzanne and

Bubba are both equally precious to God. As you get to know them and try to understand them, they'll probably end up equally precious to you too.

Kids are people. And, as with other people, sometimes you'll have good times with them and sometimes you'll have bad. Sometimes you'll end up flat on your back on the floor with all of them on top of you. And from the bottom of that giggling heap, you'll thank God for moments like this.

Other times you'll end up collapsed on the couch, your nerves in shreds after an evening of screams, disobedience, and back talk. Talk to God then too. Ask Him to help you forgive.

You see, kids are people. You can't remind yourself of that too often. And the best way to deal with them is the way God deals with all His people. Love—and forgive—them because of the love He gives to us.

9
Your Bag of Tricks

Would Mighty Mortal leap into the air without his magic cape? Would Chef Yummier go near a kitchen without salt and pepper? Would Dr. Snipandsew rush to a patient's aid without his little black bag?

Of course not. Most professionals wouldn't be caught without the tools of their trade. But many baby-sitters come to the job armed with nothing more than their bare hands.

That's because they often don't realize that their trade *has* tools. It does. You too can wade into the fray complete with a bag of tricks—literally.

Wise sitters prepare their own bag to take with them on jobs. It can be anything from a tote to a plain brown paper sack. Some sitters even decorate their bags specially to appeal to kids.

Paint or crayon on brown paper looks

cheerful (although the paper may not hold up long if you're really busy). Felt glued to a canvas or cloth tote (or shapes cut from iron-on patches) is more durable. Or, you can paint on canvas.

No matter how your bag looks, though, it's what's inside that is important. This might include coloring books, crayons, storybooks, videotapes, puzzles, toy cars, games, a stuffed toy, or anything else you think the children might enjoy.

And there's no reason why some of these things can't be religious. Religious bookstores are crammed with items especially for children. We'll go into more detail about some of them later.

"But all the kids I sit for have plenty of toys of their own," you might say. Ah, yes. But those are old, familiar toys. Kids are always fascinated by something different, something that belongs to someone else.

Remember how you used to feel when you were small and visited someone's house for the first time? You probably couldn't *wait* to see what goodies *those* kids had.

You don't have to spend a lot on your bag of tricks either. Sometimes stuff left over from your own childhood will do very well. Toys needn't be *new* to appeal to children— just different.

Besides, you can always make things—such as puppets. Lunch-size paper bags can be trimmed and decorated into really cute biblical characters. Draw on faces. Curl construction paper for hair and beards (or use cotton for older characters). Paste on fabric or gift wrap for robes. And add any other little touches that seem a good idea to you at the time.

Noah puppet with cotton hair

Noah

Esther puppet with paper hair, button earrings, and macaroni necklace

Esther

Donkey

Donkey puppet
with yarn mane

You can use puppets such as these to tell the children Bible stories. Or, let the kids act out the stories with you. Older children might even enjoy learning how to make puppets of their own.

You can easily make another sort of puppet from a pair of old socks and a few scraps. First, stuff one sock into the toe of the other. Place your hand in the outer sock, with your fingers extending up into the toe (above the inner sock), and your thumb extending downward into the heel. You've now formed the puppet's head and lower jaw.

Sew on two matching buttons for eyes and a smaller, different button for a nose.

44

Make a hat, tie, tongue, or whatever you like from scraps of felt or other cloth. Yarn hair or a fancy bow can transform your puppet into a girl.

Basic sock puppet

Decorated sock puppet

And what do you end up with? Who knows? It can be a dragon, a sea serpent, a worm, a dinosaur, or whatever you want it to be. Just give it a name and introduce it to the children.

Don't worry about not being a professional ventriloquist either. Hold the puppet some distance from your face and make your voice higher or lower when you speak for it. No one will notice—or care—that your lips are moving or that the voice is coming from you.

Before you know it, the kids will accept Snuffers (or whoever) as a real person. Sometimes they'll even tell it things they wouldn't dream of saying to you!

The simplest materials often turn out to be the best toys of all. A blank pad of paper can provide hours of enjoyment for kids. Do you know how to fold paper into a hat or a boat or a whatever? Do it for the kids. Then show them how.

Have you ever folded and cut paper to make snowflakes or doilies or Christmas trees or a line of paper dolls? What's old stuff to you may be a brand-new game for the children you're watching.

Can you draw—at all? Kids love to have older people teach them to draw even the simplest things. Here are a few starters.

A sheep

A shepherd

An angel

Now, how might you put those figures together to illustrate a Bible story?

Children also enjoy drawing stained glass windows—and it's simple. Have them start by using a pencil to make a big squiggly design on a piece of paper. Then have them color in the spaces with various colors of crayon or marking pen. Finally, have them go over the pencil lines with black crayon or marking pen. It's a stained-glass window! Now all you have to do is get an old cardboard box and make a church ...

Beginning of a stained-glass window

"Me-dolls" are fun too. If you can get huge sheets or a roll of blank paper, great. Otherwise you can tape regular newspaper pages together. Let the child lie down on the paper and draw around him or her with a dark marking pen. Cut out your drawing and have the child fill in face, hair, clothes, etc.

Then there's string. Do you know how to make a cat's cradle—or any of those other mysterious string creations? Do it for the kids. They'll beg you for encore after encore.

What else do you remember liking to do when you were small? Chances are your small charges will like it just as much.

Many sitters have found one other item very useful in their bag of tricks—a notebook. In it they keep a special page for each child. This page includes name, age, likes and dislikes, favorite stories, favorite prayers, neat things that have happened in the past, etc.

A quick review of these pages can help you feel right on top of the situation when you return to a home where you haven't been for a while—especially if you do a lot of sitting for a lot of different kids.

Your sitter's notebook is also a good place to keep that checklist of questions you should be asking each new family, as well as the pages of emergency numbers we'll talk about later.

Good grief! This sure means an awful lot of work! Is that what you're thinking by now? Well, in a way you're right. You may spend a few hours putting together your bag of tricks and notebook. And you probably won't earn any more money with them than you would have without. But you will earn more in other ways. Sooner or later, you'll begin to see the kids' eyes light up when they see you coming. You just might have as much fun with the puppets and other projects as they do. You'll know that old-fashioned (but still wonderful) feeling of a job well done.

Above all, you'll know that you've given your best to a ministry that in the long run you are doing for God

10
Play Time

In a way, it's another of the perqs of baby-sitting. You get *paid* to play.

True, the games might not be those you'd choose to play with your friends. But that doesn't mean they can't be fun (especially if you can forget for a while how old and dignified you are).

Some sitters think they can get by with plopping on the couch and telling the kids to go play by themselves. And there might be times when children really do prefer to play alone.

But usually kids love to have you join in their games. It makes everything so much more fun. (You remember, don't you?) And when the kids are having more fun, you're doing a better job, which is what you want— isn't it?

Play time can also give you a chance to

do some religious education with your charges—painlessly. As long as you know the family is Christian, you don't have to worry too much about crossing denominational lines. Most children's games (including those that follow) work just as well for little Lutherans, Methodists, Roman Catholics, or whatevers.

So here are some suggestions. You can probably add more ideas of your own.

Baby Games

Peekaboo

Sure, you know that one. You cover your face with your hands and say "All gone!" Then move your hands away and say "Peekaboo!" And baby shrieks with delight.

So make just one addition. When you move your hands away, say "Peekaboo! God loves you!"

Will baby understand? Maybe. Maybe not. You never know.

Patacake

That's an old favorite too. And, with just a few changes, you have:

Patacake, patacake, God's own child.
(Clap child's hands together.)
Mix up a cake all woolly and wild.
(Make stirring motions with child's hands.)
Roll it and toss it and give it a prod.
(Perform these actions with child's hands.)
Then bake it and say a prayer of thanks to God.
(Place palms of child's hands together.)

Here's a Foreheadthumper

This is an old German game (and it sounds very impressive indeed in German). Touch the child in the right place as you name each body part. As you say the last line, gently tickle the child.

Here's a foreheadthumper,
And here's an eyeblinker,
And here's a noseschnuffler,
And here's a mouthgrinner,
And here's a chinchinner,
A-n-n-n-d God made them all!

Action Poems

Preschoolers get a real charge out of these. They aren't hard to invent either. See if you can come up with some of your own.

The Good Samaritan

A man on a highway a long time ago
Was taking a trip down to old Jericho.
    (Make walking motions with fingers.)
Some robbers attacked him and left him half
       dead,
His body all aching, a bump on his head.
    (Rub head and moan.)
Along came a priest, and he passed right on by.
"I can't stop to help him. Oh no, no! Not I!"
    (Shake head vigorously.)
Now next came a Levite, and he passed by too.
"I simply can't stop! I have too much to do!"
    (Shake head again.)
At last a Samaritan came riding by.
He bandaged the poor man so he wouldn't die.
    (Pretend to wind bandages.)
Then on his own donkey took him to an inn
And paid for his care till he felt well again.
    (Wave arms and stamp feet.)

Jesus and the Storm

A little wooden boat was floating on the deep.
> *(Make wavelike motions with hands.)*

Jesus' friends were talking. Jesus was asleep.
> *(Pretend to be asleep.)*

Then rain began to fall. First came the little
drops.
> *(Wiggle fingers and move hands downward.)*

Then the middle-sized ones. Last came the
great big plops.
> *(Cover head.)*

The wind began to blow. It blew and blew and
blew.
> *(Make wind noises.)*

The waves began to grow. They grew and
grew and grew.
> *(Raise hands above head.)*

Now Jesus' friends were scared. They
thought their boat would tip.
> *(Lean way to one side.)*

They started calling out, "Please, Jesus, save
our ship!"
> *(Cup hands at mouth as if calling.)*

So Jesus stopped the wind. He made the
waves get small.
> *(Raise hands above head, then lower them.)*

And to His friends He said, "I'll take care of
you all."
> *(Spread arms wide.)*

The 10 Men

In Jesus' day there lived 10 men.
They all were very sick.
    (Hold up 10 fingers.)
"Jesus, You're our Friend!" they cried.
"Help us get well quick."
    (Hold up hands as if pleading.)
So Jesus made them well again,
And nine men ran away.
    (Make running motions with fingers.)
Just one told Jesus, "Thank You, Lord!"
He shared God's love, I'd say.
    (Hold up one finger.)

Motion Games

Although it may seem as if kids can sit glued to a TV set for hours, the time does come when they simply *have* to move around. When your charges reach that point, try some of these games.

Mother, May I?

It's the old game with a new twist. One person is the leader and tells the others to perform various actions. In this case, though, make them religious actions.

    "Caitlin, bow your head."
    "Sam, sing a hymn."
    "Sabrina, kneel down."

Of course the person is supposed to say, "Mother, may I?" before performing the action. Whoever forgets is out of the game. And the last person remaining gets to be leader in the next game.

Here We Go 'Round the Mulberry Bush

Another old favorite—but instead of acting out the usual verses ("This is the way we wash the clothes," etc.), try some of these:

"This is the way we go to church,
Go to church, go to church.
This is the way we go to church
So early in the morning."

"This is the way we say a prayer …"

"This is the way we sing to God …"

"This is the way we hear God's Word …"

Can you think of more verses?

Bible Story Charades

You probably won't play this one with two teams as you usually do, unless you're sitting for a *lot* of kids. But one person can think of a Bible story and act it out for the others to guess.

Quiet Games

When you think you can't possibly move another muscle, it's time to switch to some quiet games. Here are a couple.

I'm Thinking of Something

Everybody sits down. Then you look around the room, choose an object, and say, "I'm thinking of something in God's world, and it's (blue or funny or huge or whatever)."

I'm thinking of someone in God's world and she's **exhausted!**

The other players take turns guessing what you're thinking of. Whoever guesses right gets to be the next thinker.

Add-on Story

The rules for this game are simple too. You make up the beginning of the story.

"Once upon a time, there was a little boy who was afraid of milk shakes. Milk shakes scared him silly.

"One day he had to go to the ice cream parlor with his mother. There on the counter stood a huge milk shake. The little boy took one look at it and ..."

Stop and let one of the children continue the story. After he or she has carried on the action for a while, let another child take over.

You can go on taking turns in this game until you're all out of ideas—or giggling so hard that you can't talk.

Now that you've got a few games to start you off, do some thinking of your own. What games do *you* remember from *your* childhood?

11
Story Time

"Tell me a story!"

It's one of the most ancient chants of childhood. Kids will promise almost anything for a story—to brush their teeth, to go to bed, maybe even to eat their parsnips.

Story time is also a good way to quiet kids down after a bout of rough-and-tumble. Or, to put them in the mood for bed. Something about a voice spinning on and on makes their pillow seem less like the enemy.

If you enjoy making up and telling your own tales, by all means do it. Kids are immensely flattered by original, just-for-us stories.

But they won't be disappointed if you read or tell them other people's stories. And, when you stop to think about it, some of the best and most exciting stories in the world are in the Bible.

Whether you're reading or telling a tale, there are a few simple tricks that can make it more fun for the kids—and you.

Use different voices for different characters. Make them *very* different—super high, rumbly low, slo-o-ow as molasses, super quick.

You can also use your voice to build suspense. Make it softer and more intense at scary moments. Then, when the action gets hot and hairy, let yourself go!

Insert sound effects at appropriate points in the story. "Then the thunder crashed. *Rumble-BOOM!* The lightning flashed. *Ziggety-zizzety-JAG!* The waves beat against the little boat. *SLOSH! SLOSH!* Boy, were Jesus' friends scared then!"

Fun, isn't it?

Be sure to let the kids see all the pictures when you're reading from a book. Small children like to stop right in the middle of a story and talk about what they see.

"What's that, Christopher?"

"An elephant."

"And who's that behind the bush?"

"Adam."

Sooner or later, some child is going to ask you a question that makes your toes curl.

"Where did Noah put all the animals?"

"Why didn't Jesus kill the bad guys?"

Think carefully before you answer. And don't be afraid to admit it when you don't know something. Tell the kids you'll find out—maybe from your pastor—and let them know the next time you come. (Just don't forget to do it.)

Do you remember playing dress-up in cast-off grown-up clothes when you were little? Fun, huh? Or, if you never did it, now's the time to start. See what old stuff you can find around the house and drag it along with you. (You may want to wait till at least the second time you sit for a family.)

Then choose a Bible story, divvy up the roles with the kids, and use what you have as costumes. Someone should read the story aloud first, so everyone has the facts straight. Then let yourselves go and act it out.

If you're choosing a Bible story book for your bag of tricks, you'll want to keep a few points in mind.

1. The stories should agree with your church's point of view. Most will be simplified versions of what's in the Bible. But be sure the simplified versions don't wander away from the truth.

2. The pictures should be bright, colorful, and true. True pictures? Well,

remember that Jesus lived in the Middle East. We don't know exactly what He looked like. But we can be pretty sure He didn't have blond hair and blue eyes.

3. The book should be sturdy and well made. You don't want one of your charges to eat it when you're not looking.

Your religious bookstore should have plenty of books to choose from. The following list from Concordia Publishing House might help.

For Children Ages 2–5

Hear Me Read Bible Stories Series
    by Mary Manz Simon

What Next? (Creation)
Drip Drop (Noah's Ark)
Jibber Jabber (The Tower of Babel)
Hide the Baby! (The Birth of Moses)
Toot! Toot! (The Fall of Jericho)
Bing! (David and Goliath)
Whoops! (Jonah and the Fish)
Send a Baby (Birth of John the Baptist)
A Silent Night (Christmas)
Follow That Star (The Wise Men)

Row the Boat (Jesus Fills the Nets)
Rumble, Rumble (Jesus Feeds the Crowd)
Who Will Help? (The Good Samaritan)
Sit Down (Mary and Martha)
Come to Jesus (Jesus Blesses the Children)
Too Tall, Too Small (Zacchaeus)
Hurry, Hurry! (Jesus Enters Jerusalem)
Where Is Jesus? (Easter)

My Bible Story Book
    by Sarah Fletcher

*My Bible Stories with Sing-Along Songs
and Cassette*
    by Carol Greene

For Children Ages 4–9

PassAlong Arch Book Series
    by Carol Greene

God's Good Creation
Noah's Floating Zoo
Baby Moses' River Ride
Moses and the Freedom Flight
Journey to the Promised Land
David and the Dreadful Giant
Jonah's Fishy Adventure
Daniel in the Dangerous Den
Baby Jesus, Prince of Peace

Jesus Stills the Storm
Jesus' Big Picnic
Jesus and Jairus' Little Girl
Jesus and the Little Children
Jesus and the Grumpy Little Man
God's Easter Plan

Arch Book Series
        by various authors

The Story of Creation
Caleb, God's Special Spy
Samuel and the Wake-Up Call
Samson
The Fall of Jericho
Daniel and the Roaring Lions
Baby Jesus Is Born
My Merry Christmas Arch Book
Mary's Christmas Story
Three Presents for Baby Jesus
The Prodigal Son
Jesus Blesses the Little Children
My Happy Easter Arch Book
My Happy Birthday Book

12

The Sound of Music

What kind of music do you like? Chances are the kids you're watching will like it too.

They haven't had much chance to form their own musical tastes yet. So they'll probably enjoy "Blizzard" by The Fat Turtle as well as Vivaldi's "The Four Seasons." (Be sure to get permission from parents, though, before using sound equipment in the homes you're visiting.)

What children enjoy most of all is making music themselves. It's a great way to entertain them—and you—while you're sitting. Of course, if you can accompany the songs you sing on guitar, ukelele, Autoharp, piano, or whatever, all the better. But a little enthusiastic warbling on your part (with the emphasis on enthusiastic) is really all it takes to get the kids going.

You might even consider making some

rhythm instruments to carry along in your bag of tricks. Oatmeal cartons or coffee cans covered with gift wrap make good drums. Use unsharpened pencils for drumsticks. Other small containers with plastic lids make delightfully noisy shakers when you put unpopped corn or pebbles in them. And a few jingle bells sewed to an elastic wristband will give you all the Christmas spirit—even in July.

Small children love to make up actions to go with the songs they're singing. The songs that follow will give you some ideas, but you can easily make up more on your own.

Older children often like to make up new words for songs they already know. For example, to the tune of "Old MacDonald Had a Farm," sing:

God made such a pretty world.
 E - I - E - I - O
And in that world He put some ducks.
 E - I - E - I - O
With a quack-quack here and a quack-quack
  there,
Here a quack, there a quack, everywhere a
  quack-quack.
God made such a pretty world.
 E - I - E - I - O
(Of course the stanzas can go on forever.)

Then there's "Mary Had a Little Lamb."

Peter had a little boat,
Little boat, little boat.
Peter had a little boat.
He went to catch some fish.

Your turn! Try making up some songs with the children. And try learning some of these songs together.

Thank You, Loving Father

What else did God make? All the cows that moo? All the donkeys too?

Sts. 1–4 Arthur W. Gross
Sts. 5–6 Daniel Burow

Arr. Theo. J. Koch

1. God made all the food we eat;
3. God made all the birds that sing;
5. God made me and God made you;

Thank You, lov - ing Fa - ther.

2. God made all the flow'rs so sweet;
4. God made us and ev - 'ry - thing;
6. God made fa - thers, moth - ers too;

Thank You, lov - ing Fa - ther.

Praise Him, Praise Him

This song easily lends itself to new words: "Thank Him," "Love Him," "Tell Them."

Anonymous, c. 1890   Carey Bonner, 1859–1938

Setting: Copyright © 1975 Concordia Publishing House.

71

Jesus Is My Special Friend

This song is especially good for skipping or dancing.

Daniel Burow   Carol Greene

1. Je - sus is my spe - cial Friend; He goes wher - e'er I go. When I'm bad, it makes Him sad, But still He loves me so.
2. Je - sus is my spe - cial Friend; My Help - er kind and true— Night and day, at work and play, And He is your Friend too.

Tender Jesus

Children who already know this prayer might enjoy singing it at bedtime.

G. A.   Gretchen Anderson

Gently

Ten - der Je - sus, meek and mild,

Look on me, a lit - tle child.

Help me, if it is Your will,

To re - cov - er from all ill.

Table Prayer

Here's another sing-along prayer.

E. S.

Elizabeth Sparrow

Not too fast

Dear Lord, hear us pray:

Bless our food to - day.

Lord, we pray a - gain:

Bless us too. A - men.

Good Night

Can you make up additional stanzas for this song?

Victor Hugo
Carol Greene

Good night! Good night! Far flies the light; But still God's love Shall shine a - bove, Mak - ing all bright; Good night! Good night!

Little Children, Can You Tell?

This old favorite would work well at Christmas. But you might try it in August too.

Why the an - gels sing for joy
Why the an - gels sing for joy
This the won - d'ring an - gels see

On the Christ - mas morn - ing?
On the Christ - mas morn - ing.
On the Christ - mas morn - ing.

My Savior Lives

Any day is a good day to celebrate Jesus' resurrection!

Carol Greene

L. v. Beethoven, adapted

Jesus Loves the Little Children

Kids love to march around the room as they sing this song. It's also a natural for their rhythm instruments.

C. H. Woolston

George F. Root
Arr. Charlotte Mitchell

1. Je - sus loves the lit - tle chil - dren,
2. Je - sus died for all the chil - dren,

All the chil - dren of the world; Red and
All the chil - dren of the world; Red and

yel - low, black and white, All are pre - cious in His
yel - low, black and white, All are pre - cious in His

sight: Je - sus loves the lit - tle chil - dren of the world.
sight: Je - sus died for all the chil - dren of the world.

Jesus Loves Me, This I Know

And here's probably the most favorite old favorite of all.
Remember?

Anna B. Warner

William B. Bradbury
Arr. Charlotte Mitchell

1. Je - sus loves me, this I know,
2. Je - sus loves me, He who died

For the Bi - ble tells me so;
Heav - en's gate to o - pen wide;

Lit - tle ones to Him be - long,
He will wash a - way my sin,

They are weak, but He is strong.
Let His lit - tle child come in.

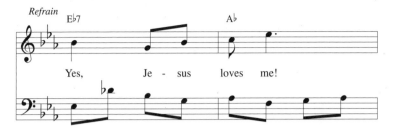

Yes, Je - sus loves me!

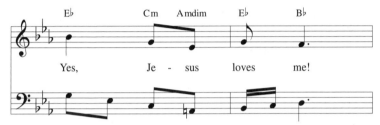

Yes, Je - sus loves me!

Yes, Je - sus loves me! The

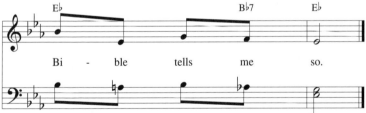

Bi - ble tells me so.

And don't forget all the other favorite
songs that you and the kids know!

13
Prayer Time

You'll want to be a little sensitive when it comes to the matter of prayers—especially if the children you're watching are of another faith. But if they go to your church, you can be pretty sure that the prayers you like will be fine for them too.

If the children know regular bedtime prayers and mealtime graces already, by all means let them use them. But you can also teach them new ones (to surprise Mom and Dad).

Use some you remember from your childhood. Or, try some of these:

> Loving Jesus, gentle Lamb,
> In Thy gracious hands I am.
> Make me, Savior, what Thou art.
> Live Thyself within my heart.
> *(Charles Wesley)*

Father in heaven,
be with all the people
who take care of me—
my Mommy and Daddy,
my brothers and sisters,
my Grandma and Grandpa,
my aunts and uncles and cousins,
and my baby-sitters.
I'm glad they love me.
(Lois Walfrid Johnson)

Teach me, my God and King,
In all things Thee to see,
That what I do in anything,
To do it as for Thee.
(George Herbert)

All good gifts around us
Are sent from heaven above.
Then thank the Lord, Oh, thank the Lord,
For all His love.
(Jane Montgomery Campbell)

Thank You for the food we eat.
Let children everywhere
Have just as much to thank You for.
Please, God, hear our prayer.
(Sarah Fletcher)

Be near me, Lord Jesus; I ask You to stay
Close by me forever and love me, I pray.
Bless all the dear children in Your tender
    care
And fit us for heaven to live with You there.
(Cradle Song)

You might also want to look at the following books from Concordia Publishing House:

God, I've Gotta Talk to You (Arch Book)
    by Walt Wangerin Jr. and Anne Jennings
Prayers for Little People by Sarah Fletcher
God's Children Pray by Mary Manz Simon

14

Discipline ...

Or, How to Get Kids to Do What They Don't Want to Do or Stop Doing What They Want to Do

Sounds like a tall order, doesn't it? Well, don't start nibbling your nails just yet. A few hints should help you trim it down to size.

Did you ever notice that the words *discipline* and *disciple* are a lot alike? And *disciple* means "follower."

H-m-m-m. If you could just get the kids to *follow* your wishes because they want to, your discipline problems would be solved.

But how can you do that?

Let's start with a few dos and don'ts.

1. *Don't* be an ogre. There's something about hearing orders barked at them

that makes a lot of people—including kids—just *have* to rebel. Don't set yourself and the kids up like that. Besides, no one loves an ogre.

2. *Don't* be wishy-washy. "O-h-h-h, I don't know. Maybe you sort of oughtn't to do that—huh?" Faced with that limp-noodle attitude, any red-blooded kid is going to get by with all he or she can.

3. *Do* refer to parents' guidelines. If Mom and Dad said no TV after 9:00, let the kids know that you consider that rule carved in stone. Most likely they'll agree with you, especially since Mom and Dad aren't around to be whined at.

4. *Don't* lose your cool. The minute you burst into tears—or fall on the floor and scream and kick your heels—the kids have won. Your job is to be on top of the situation—always, even if you suspect you're going mad.

5. *Don't* go to extremes. Sitting Charlie in the corner for two hours is *too* much. And never, *ever* use physical punishment, such as hitting a child. Your ultimate threat should be, "If you don't do that (or stop doing that), I'm going to

have to tell your parents." Use this threat sparingly. But if you do use it, follow through.

6. *Do* try humor sometimes. It's one of God's greatest gifts to us. Sometimes a mock-serious statement such as "If you don't brush your teeth right now, I'm going to put you in the encyclopedia" does wonders. Especially if you follow it up with a stern "March!"

7. *Don't* be sarcastic with the kids or put them down. You may win temporarily, but it's a cheap victory. Sarcasm and other hurtful words open wounds and destroy children's trust in you. You don't want to do that.

In the long run, you'll find that you have the fewest discipline problems with the kids who like you best—the kids who respect you and really want your approval. And that's not so unusual. Isn't it how *you* react to the people responsible for you? Take another look at chapter 8. Kids *are* people.

Sometimes you can almost feel the magic happen. One minute the struggle is still on—the struggle to determine who's in charge. The next minute you say or do something right and—presto! You've won.

15
Emergency!

Okay, they do happen sometimes—honest-to-goodness emergencies. And you're in charge. You have to cope.

Sure, that's a scary thought. But a little thinking ahead, a little planning of what you would do *if,* can make all the difference.

It can mean you won't panic. It can mean you'll make the best possible decisions. It can mean—sometimes—the difference between life and death.

So let's think ahead a bit. What would you do in case of an emergency?

First, you'd want to make sure it's a real emergency. Suppose two kids are fighting over which TV program to watch. That's no emergency. If you call Mr. and Mrs. Jones away from their gourmet dinner at a romantic restaurant to solve that sort of problem, you aren't much of a sitter.

But what if you suddenly have to cope with a seriously ill or hurt child, a fire, or a suspected prowler outside? Those are emergencies.

Say a prayer. It needn't be fancy. "Lord, help me" will do. Of course, He *will* help you—whether you ask or not. But saying that prayer helps *you* remember that He's there with you.

Stay calm. Even if your insides are quivering like Jell-O, wear a cool, competent mask on the outside. You owe that to the kids. And it'll probably help you *feel* calmer too. (One trick that sometimes works is to pretend that you're your own mother or father and to act the way you think she or he would in this situation.)

Get human help. No one expects you to handle a serious emergency alone. Remember those phone numbers the parents gave you? Use them.

Some areas have an all-purpose emergency number (such as 911) to use for fire, police, ambulance, etc. If you live in such an area, be sure you know that number.

At the end of this chapter, you'll find a page on which to write all sorts of emergency numbers. Make copies of it—one for every family for which you sit.

Ask parents to fill out the sheet the first

time you work for them. Then keep it in your sitter's notebook. Or, carry it with you each time you go to that home.

Use common sense. Sometimes things happen that you can't plan for.

Suppose a candle suddenly explodes and flames begin creeping up the wall.

That really did happen to one sitter. The parents had lit the candle in their dining room and then had forgotten about it. The first the sitter knew that there was trouble was when the six-year-old yelled, "The dining room's on fire!"

It was a freezing-cold winter night. But the sitter's common sense told her that fire was far more dangerous than cold.

So, without waiting to put on coats, she got herself and the child out of that house and to a neighbor's. From there she dialed 911.

The fire engines arrived in time to prevent any major damage. And two grateful parents couldn't stop praising the sitter for her quick—and sound—thinking.

Here are a few more hints to help you handle—or avoid—emergency situations.

1. Know where all the phones are in the house so you can call from the nearest one, if necessary.

2. Know how to operate the locks on the doors. This is especially important if a house has deadbolt locks that must be opened with a key from the inside too. Be sure you know exactly where those keys are.

3. Keep all doors and windows locked. Don't let in anyone except the children's parents—or your own.

4. Keep dangerous items (knives, medicines, matches, cleansers, etc.) out of the children's reach.

5. Don't leave any potential source of fire unwatched. This includes candles and cooking food.

6. Try to keep small children where you can see them every moment (unless they're asleep).

7. Know where the family keeps their first-aid kit. Not all emergencies are biggies. You can probably doctor a scraped elbow or knee without calling the paramedics.

8. If you're worried or have a question about something, remember that you can always call *your* parents. After all, they know a lot about taking care of kids. Look what a good job they did with you!

Emergency Checklist

Family name: _____

Father at work: _____

Mother at work: _____

Where we'll be tonight: _____

_____

Phone: _____

A relative to call: _____

_____

Pediatrician: (Office: _____)

(Exchange: _____)

Fire: _____

Police: _____

Ambulance: _____

Poison hotline: _____

All-purpose
emergency number: _____

Other numbers:
( ): _____

( ): _____

( ): _____

( ): _____

Location of first-aid kit: _____

_____

A Prayer for You

God, You've called me to serve You
By watching over some of Your children.
Help me take this ministry seriously.
Give me all those things I'll need to do it well—
Patience, kindness, cheerfulness, wisdom,
A true sense of responsibility, and humor.
Be with me during the good times
And during the hard times.
Guide me, support me, and use me as You will.
God, bless the children.
God, bless me.
In Jesus' name. Amen.